Prayers for
the Darkness

Encounters with God
When Faith Feels Powerless

PAUL MAXWELL

TABLE OF
CONTENTS

Part I
Encounters

False Prophet   2

Phoenix   3

Proof   4

Pause   5

Sir   6

Cliché   7

Click-Bait Healing   8

Unlivable   9

Help   10

Silent Passivity   11

Pretend   12

I Would, If   13

Awkward Silence   14

Magic Words   15

Not a Middle-Finger   16

Irrelevant, But Inevitable   17

If It Were Up To Us   18

$20,000   19

Cigar Intimacy   20

An Honest Psalm 119   21

Someone You're Not   22

Bully Life on Our Behalf   23

When Truth Feels False   24

A Mantra.   25

"It's Going to Be Okay"   26

The Desert Still Sucks   27

Envy   28

Pulling The Rug Out   29

A Stern Father   30

Off-Track   31

Stolen from Me   32

Pre-Social Media Faith   33

Clenched Fists   34

No Points for Style 35

Part II
Sunrise

Sunrise: Daydreams 38

Sunrise: Accuser 39

Sunrise: Show Yourself 40

Sunrise: Lost at Sea 41

Sunrise: Chokehold 42

Sunrise: Despair 43

Sunrise: Monday 44

Sunrise: For Christ's Sake 45

Sunset: Regret 46

Sunset: Medicated 47

Part III:
"The Church"

Power 50

Sunrise: Unbelonging 51

Sunday: Lost 52

Sunday: Inauthentic 53

Sunday: Clique 54

Sunday: Your Friends   55

Sunday: Untrue   56

Sunday: Easter's Not-Yet   57

Sunday: Easter's Thumb   58
in The Eye

Part IV:
Quotes

A Lifetime   60

Son of a Bitch   61

Breaks   62

Truths   Voltaire

Faith   64

Mmhmm   65

The Sky Is Empty   66

Trust a Church Bell   67

Part V:
Fleeting Thoughts

False Hope   70

Is It's Not Hard   71

Uniformed   72

World, Place, Body   73

Section VI:
Scripture

Reward   75

Lesson   76

Brand   77

Disguise   78

Introduction

God doesn't have a category for "taboo." We have been trained to think of God as the best of all possible systematic theologians. There has never been a time in human history when God spoke, and the church didn't try to use that speech as a means to control other humans — as a way to say:

> "You can't say that."
> "You can't do that."
> "You have to do what *I* say."
> "You have to feel the emotions
>   that *I* understand."

No. This deeply betrays the heart of God in his moving toward us — in his speaking to us. God desires to encounter, not our best selves, but our *true* selves. God doesn't know us by means of our resume packet, with photoshopped pictures and a highlight reel of our best moments. God sees it all. And he wants us entirely, nothing lacking, nothing overseen, nothing forgotten.

Our prayer life should reflect this. In spurning presumption, the fog of pretense is cleared between God and us, and we are able to approach him as seems fitting to us — to engage him in battle, to critique his character, to curl up into a ball and cry, to hurl profanities at him. We have been so conditioned to believe that we are responsible for how those in authority over us *feel* (though we aren't), often our prayers are formulated to protect God's feelings.

But they shouldn't be. He can handle all the "blasphemies" and "heresies" stirring around in our hearts. Many times, there is truth in them that our

Evangelical world would rather suppress than express — it fits "the narrative" better. And we wouldn't want to disrupt the narrative.

But here's one piece of truth we've forgotten: God doesn't care about the Evangelical narrative. At least, not more than people. Not more than the *individuals* in front of us and beside us. God doesn't care about Evangelicalism *more* than he cares about you. No. He cares about you *more*. Because Evangelicalism is an idea, an institution, a bank account — *you* are made *by him*, in his image.

Prayer that is fully honest — sacred *and* profane, articulate *and* fumbling for words, distrusting of God *and* engaging with him with all our misgivings on display — this is the prayer God is after. And this is the prayer that our hearts long to pray, if we would, for a moment, allow our hearts to "go there." Go there with me. And, go further than me. Go *for yourself* into the disrespectful honesty that God desires from us more than anything.

Section 1: Encounters

False Prophet

Lord,

Silence that false prophet
of doom called Anxiety,
from a future of half-truths.

He pokes out the
spiritual eyes of
my imagination.

Restore my sight, or
remove all this barbed
wire from my path.

Phoenix

Lord,

Rekindle the fire that moved
me to discipline years ago.

Burn my distracted, tangled
laziness to ash. Teach me

the hard Phoenix path.

Proof

Lord,

Let us not take
our "highs" as
proof of growth.

Nor our "lows"
as proof of failure.

Only to live
in your moment,
this moment.

Pause

God,

Press "Pause" on
all our chaos.

Help us to:
- turn our phones off
- exhale
- close our eyes
- open them to you
- remember our strength

We are ready again for you
to press "Play" on our chaos.
We haven't blinked away
all our suffering.

But we've dislodged anxiety's
stun gun from our necks.

Restore:
- our breath to our rhythm
- our blood to our muscles
- our mental clarity
- our vigorous sense of self ... behind and without
  our digital selves.

Sir

God,

Your name is often
a barrier to us,
not a bridge.

"Father" | "Lord" | "Sir"
We might as well
say "Dear Sirs."

Be more than "Sir" to us.
Be the warm peace in our souls.
Be what we have been looking for
beneath every formality
that we tolerate.

Be "God" to us
in all the ways we need
but won't admit, and
in all the ways we want,
but can't feel.

Cliché

God,

Either make good on all those
Christian clichés about power
and victory and beauty or

rip them to shreds and
give us something better.

In pain, some of us reach for
those clichés as weapons to
fight desperation.

They're not just
tweets to us.

Cliché or not,
we need you.

Listicle Healing

God,

Our teachers click-bait us.

7 Reasons ...

... You're Doing It Wrong
... You Aren't Good Enough
... Everything Is Your Fault
... You Believe The Right Thing The Wrong Way

Heal us ...

... from teachers who need our clicks.
... from friends who betray.
... from habits that imprison.
... from blogs that condemn.
... from faith that requires too much.

In our toxic, backstabbing, imprisoning
word, give us meaningful redemption.

Hide us in your bosom from
your Nazgûl on their high horses.

Unlivable

God,

We believe
the prophecy:
"If you don't figure out
the next 20 years today,
You'll be a poor, miserable loser. Forever."

Why else would we buy
all of these books for planning,
all of these products for fulfilling,
all this tequila and porn for forgetting?

Teach us how not
to live a cringing life.
But don't deprive us.
We need you to care
like you used to, because
our world feels unlivable.

Help

Lord,

"What a mess..."
"I'm so incompetent..."

Hold my hand.
I'm itching to formulate
my future without you.

I only know one word:
"Help."

Silent Passivity

God,

We have forgotten rest
in our scramble for relaxation.

We have forgotten pleasure
in our search for orgasm.

We have forgotten life
in our strategizing about living.

We have forgotten you
in our silent passivity
about ourselves.

Do in us what you know we need.
We will furiously object now,
and thank you later.

But you knew what
you were getting
into on the cross.

Pretend

God,

Free us from our
need to pretend.

It's necessary here, in
professional Christian world.

It's odd to think it's
not necessary
with you.

Show us we are
allowed to be us
with you.

We don't get that message
much around here.

I Would, If

God,

I would love you if you
and I weren't mediated
by theological goblins.

I would trust you if
I felt like you knew
what I had to lose.

I would hope again if I
didn't have your blooper reel
playing on repeat.

I would try again if you
showed up for once
like you used to.

Give me the faith to see our future
full of love, trust, and hope,
because without faith,
they simply don't exist.

Awkward Silence

God,

Our prayers only highlight
your awkward silence.

Our failures only unveil
your heavy absence.

So we'll keep
praying and failing.

Until you act
or move.

Magic Words

God,

With the enemy
pressing hard on our windpipe,

we hope you're the
kind of God who

saves us, even if we
can't say the magic words.

Not a Middle-Finger

God,

Not all our unbelief is
high-handed rebellion.

Not all our sin is
ignorant bliss.

Not all our doubt is a
theological middle-finger.

Make us into believing,
holy, faithful people by
understanding that
repentance is not
always the solution.

Irrelevant, But Inevitable

God,

Help us to unlearn
the habit of expecting
bad news to reverse itself.

Help pus to learn
the habit of cherishing
your circumstantially irrelevant
embrace.

Both are hard to receive
but inevitable.

If It Were Up To Us

God,

If it were up to us,

We would work our hands to the bone
on worthless tasks

and relax our souls to
their deathbeds with triviality.

Shake us loose from our fruitless affections.
Even the ones we identify as "Christian."

Rekindle our childhood love of just being alive.
Snap us back into homeostasis.

Snap us out of our vicious back-and-forth
between grueling labor and empty indulgence.

$20,000

God,

If you ave us $20,000
we would squander it all.

But not as much as we would
squander our 20,000
days on earth.

Let us not spend a single
day or dollar on the
opinions of others.

Cigar Intimacy

God,

Help us to stop relying on
"professional Christians" to
do all our thinking, praying,
and boundary-drawing for us.

Give us the child-like faith that
is apathetic about every form
of "Christian prestige."

Give us the front-porch-scotch-and-cigar
intimacy with you that we know
you long for with us.

An Honest Psalm 119

God,

We are expected to
experience your word as:

Full.
Visceral.
Sufficient.
Enjoyable.
Satisfying.
Invigorating.
Enlightening.

You know where
we're going with this.
Too often, your word feels:

Dry.
Bland.
Hollow.
Nepotistic.
Fabricated.
Self-interested.

Help us to unlearn all our
expectations you never gave us.

Illumine a fresh path toward "Us" again.
I miss you, sitting here, in your word.

Someone You're Not

God,

Detach "Us" from every

brand,
logo,
slogan,
tribe,
institution,
viewpoint,
and theology

that makes you feel
like someone you're not.

Bully Life on Our Behalf

God,

Life smacks us around.
Our souls are bruised.
We are sore with our
many insufficiencies.

We have prepared for grace,
mercy, patience, love,
perseverance, and grit.

Today, we only have one
desperate prayer left
in the chamber:

Bully life back
on our behalf.

When Truth Feels False

God,

We want to believe authentically,
which feels real, but
is sometimes false.

We would believe truthfully,
which is real, but
sometimes feels false.

Meet us in the
experience we cannot conjure
that is real in fact and in feeling.

There's no other truth
or authenticity that
is worthwhile.

A Mantra.

Give us peace.
Give us patience.
Give us perseverance.

"It's Going to Be Okay"

God,

I want you to tell me:
"It's going to be okay."

I know you won't say
it when I need it.

Your silence is unsurprising.
Yet, you could do *something*.

Life is hard. I'm not sure you get that.
In my world, a loyal friend will step in.

"I have called you friends" (John 15:15).
Where are you, friend?

Waiting, with diminishing hope.

The Desert Still Sucks

God,

Even though you
led us into the desert,
the desert still sucks.

So maybe you
could do something.
Since you're here
and everything.

Envy

God,

We're wind-up toys
wound tightly
with envy.

Ease our
strangle hold on
the belts of our frenemies.

Show us how—
help us now—
to let gow.

Pulling The Rug Out

God,

I always blamed you.
But now I get it.

Pulling the rug out from
under me was a mercy.

I was running to the
courthouse with a crook.

A Stern Father

God,

Show us how faith
isn't another chore

that a stern father
wants us to complete

so that he can look
good to his friends.

Show us that you're
better than that.

Don't just tell us that
you're "glorious."
Show us why.

Show us the glory of
our reckless love that
couldn't care less about
how his love makes him look.

Off-Track

God,

We are tilted off-track.
But we grit our teeth,
take a slow, deep breath,
look to you.

...

There. Balanced.
Moving forward.

Tomorrow has time for weakness.
Today, we try painful endurance
on for size.

We often call for your love.
Today, we call for your power.

Stolen

God,

Your love's trademarked.
You healing, diluted.
Your people, cliqued.
Your word, branded.

Your self has been
stolen from my self.

Return.

Pre-Social Media Faith

God,

Reintroduce us to our faith
pre-social media; pre-poisoned.

Reacquaint us
with our bodies.

After all, you've
always wanted us
face-to-face.

Clenched Fists

God,

We've clenched our fists
for so long that our hearts
are numb.

"Let go of the controls. I love you."

Help us to hear you say that,
and to feel you want that,
again.

No Points for Style

God,

We're exhausted,
balancing between

"nagging widow" and
"not like the Pharisees."

But no prayer has ever been
"too much" or "too little" for you.

When it comes to desperation,
there are no points for style.

Part II:

Sunrise

Sunrise: Daydreams

God,

Our new day means nothing
without your new mercies.

Turn our minds from
daydreams to real life.

Make our virtue
swifter than our vice.

Sunrise: Accuser

God,

Today, the accuser
is getting dressed,
preparing for:

This morning's neglect.
This afternoon's failure.
This evening's regret.

I have no hand to play except
that you are getting dressed for:

This morning's mercy.
This afternoon's patience.
This evening's repentance.

Sunrise: Show Yourself

God,

Another day.
With our arsenal of:

- unanswered prayers.
- overwhelming tasks.
- unfuilfilled reams.

We have lost all drive to
pray, overcome, and persevere.

We're done asking you to "teach us."
Don't teach us a "lesson" today.

Show us something.
Show up, or ... something.

Untangle us from
our barbed despair
with its teeth sunk in
all our arteries of faith.

If you teach us anything today,
teach us you're not a coward:
Show yourself.

Sunrise: Lost at Sea

God,

Today, we are already:

Drowning.
Critiquing you.
Sinking to the depths.

We call it: "Lost at sea."
You call it: "A meeting with destiny."

Only time will tell
which of us is right.

Sunrise: Lost at Sea

God,

Today, we are already:

Drowning.
Critiquing you.
Sinking to the depths.

We call it: "Lost at sea."
You call it: "A meeting with destiny."

Only time will tell
which of us is right.

Sunrise: Chokehold

God,

Today's hopes are already
tangled in the enemy's schemes,
in despair.

We await the moment
you'll put the enemy's
chokehold to shame.

Sunrise:
Rhythms of Despair

God,

Our morning promises failure.
Our afternoon, insufferable work.
Our evening, a way to forget.

Uproot our daily liturgies in
which we teach ourselves
to resent you.

Replace our rhythms of despair
with habits that heal "Us"
and thereby heal us.

Turn us from people
longing for dusk's end
to a people of the dawn's
new beginning.

Sunrise: Monday

God,

The pain of Monday is the
sting of exiting the sabbath.

Honor your own design.
Make the gruel of Monday's
new momentum a haunting
growl in our enemy's ears.

Make our morning grumbles,
stretches, and yawns unafraid
and purposeful like the waking
of your growing lion cub.

Sunrise: Monday

God,

Show up today
for Christ's sake

or stop asking
us to expect you.

Are you not just
phoning it in?

It certainly feels
that way.

Show up fully, for
we are empty.

Sunset: Regret

God,

Today:

We loved all the "big"
things too much
and all the "little"
things not enough.

The future.
The paycheck.
The reputation.
The respect.

vs.

You.
Her.
Him.
Them.
Us.

Help us not resort to regret
to love the right thing
at the right time.

Sunset: Medicated

God,

It's that time of day when
all our inadequacies are
undeniable, just asking
to be medicated.

Help us find medication
in the breeze, not the bottle—

facing ourselves honestly
with mercy, not in denial
taking it out on
those we love.

Section III: "The Church"

Power

Many of God's people shut their stories inside because the church has implicitly threatened to silence the abnormal. The church hasn't yet learned to institutionally, publicly, or proactively repent of their enslavement to worldly ways of being powerful.

Sunday: Unbelonging

Church can feel like
a reminder of our
unbelonging.

But we can remind
ourselves why we
ever began to go.

Changed relationships.
Shifted perspectives.
A few goo friends.
Intimacy with God.
Softened hearts.

Lord, untangle us from
our public Christianity.
Restore us with our presence.

Remind us why we went to church
before it was required of us.

Sunday: Lost

Church ... Again.

You and I don't call
the same friends
"My people."

You and I don't call
the same place
"My home."

Give me the courage to
meet your people,
to visit your home,

and to realize that
you and I are friends
and homes to each other.

Help me to regain that sense
of your presence and love
that never seems more
lost than on Sunday.

Sunday: Inauthentic

God,

On the midst of all our
cathartic self-expression,

attending church is our genuine
but inauthentic gesture to you

that you are God.

Sunday: Clique

God,

"Church" feels like a clique willing
to sacrifice the individual
for the corporate good.

Your very opposite.
Nevertheless, we go.

Let our empty attendance be
a seed that you grow into
something more like you.

And if not, then show us
how to find what church
was supposed to be
somewhere else.

Sunday: Your Friends

God,

We don't want to
hang out with you
if it means we have

to hang out with
your really mean,
judgmental friends.

Thanks for not
making us.

Sunday: Untrue

God,

Sunday is the day we
cannot hide from
how untrue all
your words
feel all the
time.

The fact is:
We need you when
you feel most false.

Sunday: Easter's "Not Yet"

God,

Easter is a splinter.

We get it: you conquer.
And us: conquered by sorrow.

Remember:
Your Sunday "now"
is still our "not yet."

Sunday:
Easter's Thumb in the Eye

God,

To the grieving, Easter can
feel like your thumb
in our eye sockets,
not victory.

But please carry one.
We don't want to disrupt
your party's favorite cliche.

Section IV: Quotes

A Lifetime

False enchantment can
last a lifetime.
—W. H. Auden

Son of a Bitch

How are people going to tell
the difference between a person
of authentic spiritual authority
and some charismatic son of a bitch?

—Wendell Berry

Breaks

The world breaks everyone
and afterwards many are
strong at the broken places.

—Ernest Hemingway

Truths

There are truths which are not
for all men, nor for all times.

—Voltaire

Faith

Faith feels many different ways.
It can be buoyant.
It can be depressed
and lifeless.

Faith is simply
turning to the Lord.

—Ed Welch

Mmhmm

Inconsistently
crying our for
consistency.

—Relient K

The Sky Is Empty

I talk to God but
the sky is empty.

—Sylvia Plath

Trust a Church Bell

Things, they are not okay,
and I can't trust a church bell,
though I would like to.

—Ari Banias

Section V: Fleeting Thoughts

False Hope

Hope requires bravery because
false hope is cruel as Hell.

If It's Not Hard

If it's not hard,
it's not virtue.

In other words:

Evil hates beauty
and the habits
that create it.

Uniformed

God's anger seems very cruel — like a grade school bully. And then, evil becomes personal to us. And then, we need him to be angry for us.

God's love seems very good — like a childhood friend. And then, evil becomes personal to us. And then, we need him to explain himself to us.

God's action in our lives is both harsh and warm. No divine joy or bewilderment makes sense. The cross is a germ to uniformed experiences of God.

World, Place, Body

There is no world
in which God loves
us more because
we are better.

There is no place
we could go
where we belong
more than here, with him.

There is no body
we could have
that is more suited
to God's purpose for us.

Section VI: Scripture

Reward

"I will give thanks to the Lord with my whole heart; I will recount all of your wonderful deeds." (Psalms 9:1)

He doesn't wait for his heart to give thanks. He doesn't even try to feel thankful. He begins by reciting facts in grade school fashion.

The moment of authentic gratitude is not David's long-awaited prompt for intimacy with God. Authenticity *is* his reward.

Lesson

"So I hated life, for what is done under the sun is vanity. ... And in the night his heart does not rest. This too is vanity." (Ecclesiastes 2:17, 23)

Ceaseless vexation. Eye-scratching hopelessness. Shackled in meaninglessness. God speaks: It's part of the process. It takes us somewhere. No "lesson." The point is, there *is* no point:

"There is nothing better for a man than to find joy in his toil. This too is from God." (Ecclesiastes 2:24)

Brand

"The fear of man lays a snare,
but whoever trusts in
the LORD is safe."
(Proverbs 29:25)

Men brand.
They bulldoze.
God, keep my eyes on you.

Disguise

"Why, O LORD, do you stand far away? Why do you hide yourself in times of trouble?" (Psalm 10:1)

Either (1) David is wrong about God, or (2) The question "How is God showing himself to you through this trial?" is presumptive.

Not all suffering is a lesson. Not every heartbreak is God in disguise. Not all pain is encoded theology. Thank God.

To buy the book *When Your Twenties Are Darker Than You Expected*, visit Amazon. To learn more about Paul, visit paulcmaxwell.com.

Made in the USA
Lexington, KY
20 November 2017